Discovering Mission Santa Bárbara

BY JACK CONNELLY

This book was purchased with funds from a generous donation by

Dr. Kathryn W. Davis

New York

Published in 2015 by Cavendish Square Publishing, LLC
243 5th Avenue, Suite 136, New York, NY 10016

Website: cavendishsq.com

This publication represents the opinions and views of the author based on his or her personal experience, knowledge, and research. The information in this book serves as a general guide only. The author and publisher have used their best efforts in preparing this book and disclaim liability rising directly or indirectly from the use and application of this book.

CPSIA Compliance Information: Batch #WS14CSQ

All websites were available and accurate when this book was sent to press.

Library of Congress Cataloging-in-Publication Data

Connelly, Jack.
Discovering Mission Santa Bárbara / Jack Connelly.
pages cm. — (California missions)
Includes index.
ISBN 978-1-62713-100-1 (hardcover) ISBN 978-1-62713-102-5 (ebook)
1. Santa Barbara Mission—History—Juvenile literature. 2. Spanish mission buildings—California—Santa Barbara—History—Juvenile literature. 3. Franciscans—California—Santa Barbara—History—Juvenile literature. 4. Chumash Indians—Missions—California—Santa Barbara—History—Juvenile literature. 5. California—History—To 1846—Juvenile literature. I. Title.

F869.S45C67 2014
979.4'91—dc 3

2014008345

Editorial Director: Dean Miller
Editor: Kristen Susienka
Copy Editor: Cynthia Roby
Art Director: Jeffrey Talbot
Designer: Douglas Brooks
Photo Researcher: J8 Media
Production Manager: Jennifer Ryder-Talbot
Production Editor: David McNamara

Printed in the United States of America

Contents

Mission Santa Bárbara is one of the oldest missions in California.

1
Exploring a New World

Sitting on a hill overlooking the seaside city of Santa Barbara, California, is the historic Mission Santa Bárbara. Located about 90 miles (145 kilometers) north of the bustling city of Los Angeles in Southern California, Mission Santa Bárbara is a popular church and tourist destination, hosting visitors who come to pray and learn about the history of the site in its museum. The structure has stood for more than 200 years, long before the formation of the United States, back when Spanish **missionaries** and soldiers were first settling the land that would one day be California.

THE SPANISH ARRIVE

In 1492, Italian explorer Christopher Columbus accidentally discovered an area of the world called the West Indies. This was a place that had never before been seen by Europeans. His discovery led the Spanish, for whom Columbus worked, to explore the area around it. In the 1500s they found the rich, fertile land of the Americas (North, South, and Central) and the various **indigenous** tribes that lived there. The Spanish sent explorers to settle the land, along with **friars**, or priests, to **convert** the Native people. Men, including Hérnan Cortés, Juan Rodríguez Cabrillo, and Sebastián

Spanish explorers such as Hernán Cortés landed in the New World and claimed land for Spain.

Vizcaíno, claimed new land for Spain. But after a while, only the lower part of the new country, which they called New Spain, was built on and explored.

In the mid-1700s, however, Spain became eager to settle the land in the north and create a mission system. This urgency was because other countries, such as Russia and England, were building forts and villages in the area. Spain wanted to claim what is now California as its own. A mission is a religious community that teaches people about a certain religion. Other missions had been set up in the 1600s by **Jesuit** priests in lower New Spain, called Baja California. The priests had converted many of the Native people to **Christianity**. In the 1700s, **Franciscan** friars were asked to run all missions and start new ones in the upper area, called Alta California. The Spanish government thought that by converting the Native people into Spanish citizens, Spain's empire would become even larger. More explorers, soldiers, and friars helped discover the best places to build missions in Alta California, and eventually twenty-one communities were started along the coast.

The scenic area near today's city of Santa Barbara is home to one of the most beautiful Spanish missions. Mission Santa Bárbara, the tenth mission founded, was built in 1786, almost twenty years after the founding of the first mission. Its history is vast, full of triumphs and hardships, and its legacy shapes the continuing story of California today.

2
The Native Chumash

European explorers were not the first people to experience the California area. Native people had lived in the area for millennia. They set up communities, called tribes, and lived in different areas, called territories, which offered land and animals for food. When Vizcaíno visited Alta California in 1602, it is estimated that more than 300,000 Native people lived there.

The Native group associated with Mission Santa Bárbara is the Chumash. Their territory stretched from San Luis Obispo to Malibu and the Santa Monica Mountains. They had many traditions and spoke their own language.

CHUMASH VILLAGES

The Chumash lived in dome-shaped houses that could hold as many as fifty people. Each house was made of whalebone, reeds, and branches of willow trees. The buildings in the village were covered with mats of **tule**, tightly woven reeds used to keep out the wind and rain.

Every village had at least one *temescal,* or sweat lodge, where people could cleanse their bodies by sweating before a roaring fire. Afterward, they would wash themselves in the ocean or a nearby

The Chumash lived in tight-knit communities called villages.

lake or stream. This method was used before special religious ceremonies or hunting trips. Occasionally women used it, too.

SHAMANS

A chief and a **shaman** led every Chumash village. Although men usually served in the chief and shaman positions, women sometimes held these leadership roles, too. The chief was the person in charge of passing out food and valuables to the tribe members. He or she was also the leader in battles with other tribes. The biggest disputes were usually over control of land used for hunting or gathering food. The shaman was the religious leader of the community. He or she also consulted large charts of the skies. These charts were important tools in making decisions. Shamans also guided those who were sick and were often called on to locate new food sources or, in some cases, to bring rain.

CHUMASH FOOD

The Chumash did not farm but lived off the land and animals around them. They spent most days hunting, gathering, and preparing food. The women gathered fruits, nuts, herbs, and vegetables, while the men hunted for animals such as deer, bear, and fish. Acorns were a very important food source for the Chumash. They could be stored easily and for a long time. After picking acorns and finding seeds, the Chumash women used rocks to grind them into flour to make breads and other food.

CLOTHING

Men and children usually wore little or no clothing in warm weather, while women wore grass skirts. When it was colder, everyone wore coats and other clothing made of warm animal fur.

TOMOLS

The Chumash were known throughout the land for building the strongest and quickest boats, which they called *tomols*. Tomols were large and could easily hold up to ten people. They were used for fishing and traveling to nearby islands, and were among the best-crafted canoes of any Native tribe.

EDUCATION, CRAFTS, AND GAMES

All tribespeople were educated at a young age in the teachings and traditions held by their village. Older tribespeople taught the young children the skills they would need as they grew into adulthood. Boys were taught to hunt and make tools. Girls learned to weave baskets and to gather and prepare food.

Games and crafts were also important to the villagers. Most villages had a specific area for holding dances and playing games. Dancing and music were also important to the Chumash. They performed ritualistic dances and sang songs for celebrations and ceremonies.

RELIGIOUS BELIEFS AND PRACTICES

The Chumash people believed that gods could be found in all living things including people, birds, animals, and fish. They respected the land by hunting and gathering only what they needed in order to live. Along with respecting nature the Chumash worshiped the sun and moon as gods and believed in good and evil spirits.

When the Spanish eventually arrived in California to establish the mission system, the Chumash way of life was forever changed.

The Chumash built strong boats that were used to fish on the waters nearby. Some of these boats could hold ten or more people.

3
The
Mission System

The concept of a mission system existed for many centuries in other parts of Europe. When the Spanish arrived in New Spain, they brought these ideas with them. Spain's main goal there was to convert the Native people to Christianity and to expand the size of the Spanish empire. Missions helped them accomplish that goal.

CONVERTING THE NATIVE PEOPLE

The Spanish viewed the people of California as "uncivilized" because they lived their lives so differently from the Europeans and believed in multiple gods rather than one. In order to save their souls and to ensure New Spain had true Spanish citizens, the Spanish thought it was best for the Native people to adopt Spanish customs and believe in the Christian faith. The Spanish believed that the Native people would learn to appreciate the Spanish culture, religion, and manufactured goods, and that they would think of Spanish ideas and objects as superior to what they had known and used before. The Spanish held these beliefs largely because of the cultural isolation of the time. This way of thinking led to the destruction of many Native California groups and their diverse and flourishing cultures.

STARTING THE MISSIONS OF ALTA CALIFORNIA

The missions of Alta California were modeled after the Jesuit missions in Baja California. The first mission, San Diego de Alcalá, was founded in 1769 by Fray Junípero Serra, the first president, or leader, of the Alta California missions. Prior to founding the first mission, expeditions led by some of Spain's most experienced soldiers and friars searched along the coast for the perfect location. Requirements for a mission site included land that was good for growing crops and raising **livestock** close to a source of water, and close to a thriving Native population.

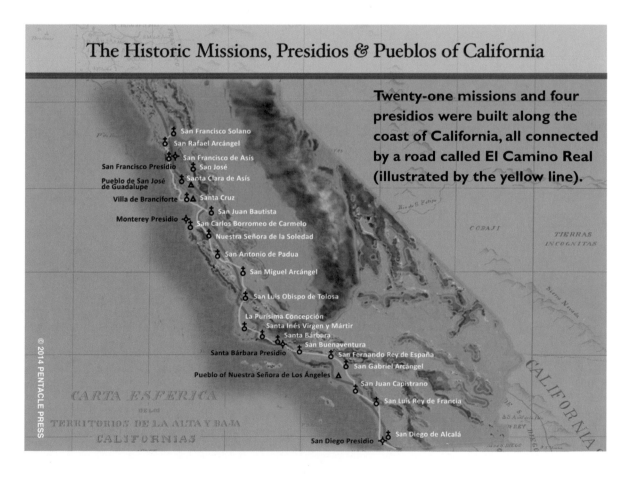

The Historic Missions, Presidios & Pueblos of California

Twenty-one missions and four presidios were built along the coast of California, all connected by a road called El Camino Real (illustrated by the yellow line).

San Francisco Solano
San Rafael Arcángel
San Francisco de Asís
San Francisco Presidio
San José
Pueblo de San José de Guadalupe
Santa Clara de Asís
Villa de Branciforte
Santa Cruz
San Juan Bautista
Monterey Presidio
San Carlos Borromeo de Carmelo
Nuestra Señora de la Soledad
San Antonio de Padua
San Miguel Arcángel
San Luis Obispo de Tolosa
La Purísima Concepción
Santa Inés Virgen y Mártir
Santa Bárbara
Santa Bárbara Presidio
San Buenaventura
San Fernando Rey de España
San Gabriel Arcángel
Pueblo of Nuestra Señora de Los Ángeles
San Juan Capistrano
San Luis Rey de Francia
San Diego Presidio
San Diego de Alcalá

© 2014 PENTACLE PRESS

CARTA ESFERICA DE LOS TERRITORIOS DE LA ALTA Y BAJA CALIFORNIAS

Like other missions, Santa Bárbara was built by the men and women who lived and worked there.

BUILDING AND RUNNING THE MISSIONS

In Alta California both soldiers and missionaries were sent to construct the missions and teach the Native people. The Native people who converted were called neophytes. They could live at the mission and would also help build mission buildings and *presidios*, or forts, where the soldiers lived and protected the people. The friars would teach them about Christianity and how to grow crops and raise livestock. The neophytes were also taught trades such as leather making, shoemaking, and blacksmithing.

LEAVING THE MISSIONS TO THE NATIVE PEOPLE

The Spanish believed it would take about ten years to train the neophytes so that they could be self-sufficient and live on their own in the new environment. Once the missionaries felt that the neophytes were ready, the mission land would be returned to them and the neophytes, now Spanish citizens, could control it.

4
Beginning Mission Santa Bárbara

The first eight missions were founded by Fray Junípero Serra between 1769 and 1777. They had all done well and were growing by the time Fray Serra searched the lands for the next missions in 1782.

FOUNDING MISSION SANTA BÁRBARA

In early 1781, Fray Junípero Serra joined an expedition led by Captain don Fernando Xavier de Rivera y Moncada, whose intent was to bring settlers from Baja California to Mission San Gabriel. The expedition to San Gabriel traveled in two separate parties: one by sea with settlers and their families, and the other by land with livestock. Eventually they all arrived at Mission San Gabriel Arcángel, though Captain Rivera and six of his men, who had been guiding the livestock, were killed before they could reach the mission. Although shaken, Serra was determined to set out on his own expedition and find new mission sites.

In March 1782, Fray Serra and Felipe de Neve, who was Spanish governor of *Las Californias* at the time, along with a group of soldiers, went to find the next mission sites and the site for the presidio. During their travels, they passed through the Santa Clara

Fray Junípero Serra is best known for founding the first missions of Alta California.

River Valley and came across land for the ninth mission, which they founded on March 31, 1782, and named San Buenaventura.

San Buenaventura was officially dedicated in 1782. Soon after, Fray Serra left one of the other friars and some soldiers in charge. From there the remaining members of the group moved on, presumably to found the tenth mission. However, Governor de Neve had other ideas. He was intent on finding a location for the presidio, and he eventually won. The presidio was founded in April 1782. Plans to build Mission Santa Bárbara were postponed until after the presidio had been built—four years later.

In 1786, a new governor, Pedro Fages, granted Fray Serra's successor, Fray Fermín Francisco de Lasuén, permission to venture into the Santa Barbara area to find land on which to build the tenth mission. The area Fray Lasuén chose was located near the Chumash village of Xana'yan, on a hilltop surrounded by rolling hills and **verdant** terrain. The mission itself was nicknamed the "Queen of Missions" because of the beautiful scenery that surrounded it. The group found the area late in 1786, and on December 4, Fray Lasuén performed a Mass—a Christian religious ceremony—and officially named the site Mission Santa Bárbara. This was one of two ceremonies to celebrate the beginning of the tenth mission. A second ceremony was held two weeks later on December 16 so Governor Fages and other important government figures could attend.

FRAY ANTONIO PATERNA AND CRISTÓBAL ORAMAS

The first friars in charge of the mission were Fray Antonio Paterna and Cristóbal Oramas. Fray Paterna was a companion of Fray Serra's, and Fray Oramas was new to the mission system. Together they ministered to the Native people, brought them to the mission site, and taught them Christianity and how to build and farm.

CONVERTING THE CHUMASH

With shelter and protection provided along with the abundance of food offered by the missionaries, Mission Santa Bárbara became an inviting place for some of the Chumash nearby. As the Chumash became comfortable with the mission, the missionaries encouraged them to be baptized into the Christian faith. The missionaries tried to get the Native people interested in Christianity by playing beautiful music and holding lovely ceremonies. Music and dance brought some of the Chumash to Christianity. The Native people enjoyed dance and music in their own religion and thus found the music played by the friars pleasurable. For this and other reasons, the Native population gradually became neophytes and lived full time at the mission.

CLOTHING

As soon as a person became a neophyte, he or she was provided clothing by the Spanish, as nudity was unacceptable to the Europeans. Once each year, men were given a new pair of pants and women received a blouse and skirt. It was very important to the friars that the neophytes adopt the cultural traditions of the Spanish people.

LIVING AT THE MISSION

Deciding to become a neophyte for some was at first exciting. People had to dedicate their lives to the mission, work very hard, and stick to a strict schedule. Once their previous religious beliefs and traditions were abandoned, the neophytes were allowed to visit their families in the Native villages. Over time, however, missionaries discovered that many neophytes continued to secretly practice the religion of their ancestors, which led to them change the mission rules: neophytes could no longer go to their villages to visit family, or practice any part of their heritage. This had damaging effects on the lives of some neophytes, and later contributed to conflict at Mission Santa Bárbara.

5
Early Days at the Mission

Construction at Mission Santa Bárbara did not start right away. In the months following the mission's first ceremony, rain hit the area. The friars and soldiers then had to stay at the nearby Santa Bárbara presidio. Finally, in March 1787, construction on the first Santa Bárbara mission buildings began. These buildings, made of simple materials like wood and *adobe*—a mixture of mud, straw, and manure—included residences for the friars, a church, and kitchens and a granary. Over the next ten years, soldiers from the presidio and neophytes at the mission completed these structures.

BUILDING A MISSION

The first buildings on the mission site were constructed in log-cabin style. Among these structures were a residence, a chapel, a kitchen, and a storeroom for grain. It was soon discovered that the materials used were too unstable to withstand the changing climates. The friars then decided to follow in the footsteps of other missions and build the structures using adobe, which they shaped into bricks and left to dry in the sun before being used. In 1789, the second church, made from adobe, was constructed. Five years later, when the mission population outgrew its adobe building, a third and larger adobe church was constructed. In 1812, the third Santa Bárbara church was damaged in an earthquake, and the missionaries decided to construct a new one of stone. Not only would it be sturdier, sandstone was plentiful in the area and could be quarried quickly. In 1815, under the direction of a different friar, Fray Antonio Ripoll, the new church was started. It was designed after a first-century-BCE Roman building. The church was completed in 1820 and stood unchanged for more than 100 years.

Throughout most of the mission period, houses for neophytes were built every year. By 1834, there were more than 200 small adobe homes that made up the neophyte village. Other structures were built around the church, forming a square with an open area in the middle. This was called a quadrangle. Workshops were built where men could do hide **tanning** or shoemaking, and women could weave and make soap and candles. Unmarried women and girls over the age of eleven were grouped together in a large room called a *monjerío*. Each night the monjerío was locked to keep the women from leaving and to prevent unwelcome guests from sneaking in. The missionaries' quarters, or living space, and a kitchen and dining area were also part of the quadrangle.

CROPS

There were several thriving crops planted and cared for at Mission Santa Bárbara, including wheat, barley, corn, beans, lentils, chickpeas, and peas. Over the years that crops were produced at the mission (1787–1823), there were reportedly 223,000 bushels of these crops collected. The mission also cultivated grapes from two large vineyards and fruit from their many fruit orchards. Although the friars initially assisted when teaching the neophytes to plant, ultimately the neophytes were held responsible for all forms of farming.

LIVESTOCK

In addition to the crops, soldiers and neophytes also cared for the animals that lived on nearby mission ranches. Cattle were especially important as they were used for food as well as milk for all the people who lived at the mission. Each animal in the herd was branded with a design unique to the mission. This design made it easy to find any cattle that went missing and to keep count of how many cattle belonged to the mission. Between 1802 and 1823, Mission Santa Bárbara had 10,000 head of livestock animals. These animals, along with the crops produced, were essential for a mission's survival.

Neophytes built an irrigation system that brought water to the mission.

WATER AND IRRIGATION

At Mission Santa Bárbara the neophytes were responsible for

Today the Moorish fountain stands as an example of the great Spanish architecture that continues to influence California.

building systems that would bring water from Pedragoso Creek, located two miles away, to the mission site. There were two stone **aqueducts** that carried the water. One would store the water in a reservoir, while the other would bring drinking and bathing water directly to the mission. This elaborate system, completed in 1806, helped the people at the mission survive. The citizens of Santa Barbara use some of the sections of this waterway today.

THE MOORISH FOUNTAIN

In 1808, carpenter and mason José Antonio Ramirez constructed a beautiful fountain close to where the final church would stand. Called the Moorish fountain, it can still be seen today. Characterized by horseshoe-shaped arches, Moorish is a style of architecture that was common in Spain from the thirteenth to the sixteenth centuries. The fountain's basin is octagonal in shape, with the actual fountain springing from the middle. It is one of the focal points of architecture at the mission and highlights the mission's rich history and unique design.

THE CHURCH

Inside the 1820 church, soft blends of orange, yellow, brown, and green cover the walls. Above the tabernacle—a box in which the holy bread and wine are kept in a Catholic church—hangs the cross of Jesus. In front of it sits an altar that was decorated by the Chumash who lived at the mission. The church serves as a witness to many of the struggles experienced in the mission's later years.

6
Daily Life

The activities at Mission Santa Bárbara were very strictly scheduled. As at other missions, the ringing of the bells regulated the day's routine. Every mission had at least two bells with different tones: the first rang when it was time to pray or have devotions, and the other signaled work, mealtimes, and rest. At Mission Santa Bárbara there are six bells that hang in two bell towers, but it is likely that prior to the final church being built in 1820, the mission had only two bells.

THE SCHEDULE

A day at Mission Santa Bárbara always began at sunrise when everyone went to the church to pray and sing. Mass was in Latin and individual prayers were in the Chumash language. An hour later, the bell rang for breakfast, a meal that usually consisted of *atole*, porridge made of thick corn and vegetables. Then the neophytes went to do their work. They ate their afternoon meal of *pozole*, a thick soup or stew, and took a rest, called a *siesta*, around midday. Two hours later, everyone returned to work. At sunset, the Chumash again attended the mission church, listening to the missionaries' prayers and Bible lessons. After church, supper was held for all, followed by free time. Free time for both adults and children usually consisted of playing games, and gambling was popular among men. A bell rang at 8 p.m., signaling bedtime for

Bells signaled when it was time to work, eat, rest, and sleep each day.

women and girls, and the final bell rang at 9 p.m., signaling bedtime for the men.

LIFE FOR NEOPHYTES

Life for the neophytes living at the mission had never been so structured. They were used to working when they needed to work and sleeping when they were tired. The missions changed that way of life and forced them to work, eat, and sleep at certain hours of the day. Often laborers worked very hard and for long hours to complete all of their assigned tasks.

While missionaries did allow neophytes to practice some of their old traditions, such as hunting, gathering, and cooking their own food, over time many neophytes became unhappy and would try to return to their villages. They were then considered runaways. The soldiers who worked at the mission usually caught and punished runaways. Punishments were also sometimes given to neophytes who did not work hard enough. This negative treatment would eventually lead to a key period of tension at the mission.

DAILY TASKS

To keep the mission running, neophytes labored at different assigned tasks. In the early days of Mission Santa Bárbara, many of the men were kept busy with its construction. Eventually neophyte men and boys looked after the fields and livestock, too. Much time was also devoted to establishing and maintaining the mission's extensive water system. Women and girls, on the other hand, completed tasks such as weaving, cooking meals, and washing clothes.

Many of the crops, such as corn and wheat, were ground down by the women and used for flour or porridge. The Chumash had been

At Mission Santa Bárbara, friars did tasks such as harvesting hay, as this photograph from 1890 shows.

grinding seeds with stone mortars—bowls made from stone that is used to grind food such as corn or seeds—long before they met the Spaniards. This technique was easily applied to mission life. Eventually iron mills were introduced, which is thought to have allowed four women to grind down the same amount of food as it took 100 women to do with the stone mortars.

Children also had jobs at the mission. Usually in the morning they would listen to the friars preach from the Bible and then in the afternoon they would help the adult neophytes with their work in the fields or with chores.

As the years passed and the mission population leveled out, many neophytes were given the task of recruiting other Native Californians into the mission system. They were sent out to their old villages, as well as to other tribal villages miles away, and ordered to bring back more converts, who were often brought against their will. We know today that the Native people's choices were not respected, and that under the mission system their freedom was unfairly violated.

LIFE FOR FRIARS AND SOLDIERS

Daily life for friars and soldiers resembled that of the neophytes, yet they were also responsible for running the mission. Friars managed the mission's funds and ensured that there was enough money, supplies, and food to survive. Soldiers had to protect the mission as well as the surrounding area and livestock. Adjusting to life in a foreign land was not easy. Eventually soldiers became unhappy and began neglecting their work and treating the Native people badly.

7
Troubles at the Mission

In one way or another, all twenty-one of the Alta California missions experienced difficulties. While Mission Santa Bárbara did not suffer from the fires and floods that plagued many of the other missions, it was not without its own dark periods. The troubles at Mission Santa Bárbara mostly involved the way the community functioned and how neophytes were treated.

PIRATES

Trouble arrived in 1818, when off the California coast French pirate Hippolyte de Bouchard threatened the town of Monterey and its presidio. One hundred and fifty neophytes from Mission Santa Bárbara trained alongside soldiers from the presidio and confronted the crew. Soon after, de Bouchard left the area without attacking.

BUILD UP TO TROUBLE

As the years passed at the missions, neophytes grew more and more discontented. They missed their families, the freedom to practice their own religion and traditions, and the lifestyle they had experienced for centuries. Many of the Native people living at the missions had endured loss of family members and friends when the Spaniards arrived. The Spanish had brought with them diseases the Native population had never before experienced. Over time, entire tribes of indigenous people died or were severely affected by terrible epidemics of smallpox and measles. This devastated neophytes and the Native population living in California. The worst outbreak of disease occurred in the winter of 1806, when a measles epidemic swept the California coast.

In addition to a difficult lifestyle and crippling illnesses, the Chumash living and working at Mission Santa Bárbara suffered at the hands of the soldiers. Often soldiers—and sometimes the friars—would mistreat neophytes, abusing them or making them work longer hours than necessary. This mistreatment increased once New Spain, then renamed Mexico, gained its independence from Spain in 1821 and mission soldiers were no longer getting paid well by the government. The soldiers worked even less and took their frustrations out on the laborers they managed.

The friars attempted to ease tensions at the mission by allowing friends and family members of the neophytes to visit them. The hope was that they would provide comfort and a sense of familiarity. Unfortunately, this proved a weak gesture and one attempted too late. The problems only escalated, and at Mission Santa Bárbara the worst came in 1824.

UPRISING

In February 1824, neophytes at Mission Santa Inés—less than fifty miles north of Santa Barbara—took action against mission soldiers

During the revolt of 1824, soldiers from the Santa Bárbara presidio faced the neophytes who had taken over the mission in a battle that cost lives on both sides.

© PENTACLE PRESS

after witnessing a visiting neophyte from La Purísima Concepción being beaten. The people had lived long enough in pain and misery, and felt it was time to retaliate. The conflict quickly spread to nearby Mission La Purísima Concepción. Word of the uprising soon reached Mission Santa Bárbara.

It was not long before neophytes at Mission Santa Bárbara decided to start their own revolt. The head friar, Fray Antonio Ripoll, wrote his own account of the uprising and described the events in detail. He and the other priests were spared since they were not the main cause of the tension. Neophyte leaders at the mission led the attack on soldiers, who were the targets of the neophytes' anger. Soon troops from the Santa Barbara presidio as well as Mission La Purísima Concepción marched toward the mission, ready to fight anyone who got in their way.

Within each mission there were various Native leaders elected by the people. These leaders were called *alcaldes*, and one of them at Mission Santa Bárbara was Andrés Sagimomatsse, who acted as the uprising's main organizer. He heard of the soldiers' intentions and ordered that all women and children move from the mission and into the safety of the hills. Sagimomatsse and several other men then grabbed weapons and prepared to attack the Spanish soldiers who were marching toward Mission Santa Bárbara. In the small battle that occurred, several Chumash and some Spanish were killed or wounded. Afterward, Sagimomatsse and other Chumash retreated to the hills to find other California Natives who would help in the fight. Despite their efforts, they were never able to organize a full-scale rebellion. After a time, a truce between the Native Californians and the soldiers was reached. Many neophytes eventually returned to the mission because they had nowhere else to go.

AFTERMATH

After the uprising subsided, attempts were made to resume life as it once had been. However, at the three missions affected, relationships between the friars, the neophytes, and the soldiers were never the same. Despite this, records from the following year, 1825, show the neophyte population at Mission Santa Bárbara having only decreased by forty-three members. This was all to change over the next ten years when the new Mexican government set their eyes on the future of Spanish missionary work in Alta California.

8
Secularization

The newly founded Mexican government wanted the rich lands of Alta California for itself. The missions of Alta California held much interest for the Mexican government. They were built on large areas of land that could be divided and given to Mexican immigrants relocating to the area.

In 1834, the Mexican government decided to secularize the missions, which means to change from religious to political rule. With the government in charge, the running of the missions would no longer require priests. The friars living there would either be sent back to Spain or kept on to minister to the spiritual needs of the community.

The plan was for some of the mission lands to be kept by the government, but for most to be handed over to the settlers and neophytes. Originally the Spanish had also intended to give the missions and its lands over to the neophytes to manage on their own. That never happened because the friars never thought the neophytes were ready.

CONSEQUENCES OF SECULARIZATION

The missionaries were against **secularization** and resisted it for as long as they could. Their entire life's work was coming to an end. Secularization also meant the people living at the missions

After secularization, Mission Santa Bárbara continued to be managed by the Franciscans.

could leave, yet many were divided about what to do. Not many neophytes by that time knew how to live on their own or how to practice any of their ancestral traditions, or even where to find their villages. Many of the Chumash had long since left the area. While many went in search of new beginnings, some neophytes remained since that lifestyle was all they knew.

A man named José Figueroa, who was governor of the California territory, was put in charge of overseeing the secularization of the missions. He had different ideas on how to divide the valuable mission lands. He never planned to turn all of it over to the Native people or immigrants. Instead, he gave much of the land to rich ranchers and government officials.

Of all the twenty-one missions, Santa Bárbara is the only one to be consistently occupied by the Franciscans. It was secularized in 1834, but remained occupied by Fray Narciso Durán, the last of the mission presidents, and acted as mission headquarters until 1846, when he died. Then-governor, Pio Pico, seized the lands and sold them to farmers. The church and mission buildings, however, remained functioning.

Today the mission is a popular tourist destination and has many interesting artifacts and buildings to explore.

9
Mission Santa Bárbara Today

Walking on the historic grounds of Mission Santa Bárbara today may feel like stepping into the eighteenth century. After suffering damage from an earthquake in 1925, much of the mission site has been restored to its original state. It continues to be operated by Franciscan friars, who continue to dress in traditional robes. The mission also acts as the main cultural and historical center for the city of Santa Barbara. It boasts a museum with authentic exhibits that display artifacts from the mission days. Tours are offered to visitors throughout the year. Efforts continue to restore key features of the mission, such as its sandstone walls and pillars.

LEGACY OF THE FRANCISCANS

The Santa Bárbara mission is one of only four missions that remain under control of the Franciscans. The other missions are San Luis Rey de Francia, San Antonio de Padua, and San Miguel Arcángel. The mission's church continues to thrive and grow, and services are held daily.

For centuries, Franciscans have been an important part of mission Santa Bárbara.

REMEMBERING THE MISSIONS

A walk through the museum allows visitors to explore rooms that have been recreated from the mission period. For instance, a friar's bedroom showcases the sparse furnishings of the times, including a bed made from an animal skin stretched tightly across a bed frame. In the kitchen, a large stone fireplace takes up much of the room, as does a table used for preparing meals of atole and pozole.

Attached to the museum and church is the cemetery. In all, there are more than 4,000 Native people buried there, including the body of Juana María, whose life story was told in the award-winning children's book *Island of the Blue Dolphins*.

While the mission system permanently altered the way of life for thousands of Native people, it also shaped California into the state it is today. Mission Santa Bárbara's legacy continues to remind all who visit that this was a place that changed lives and made history.

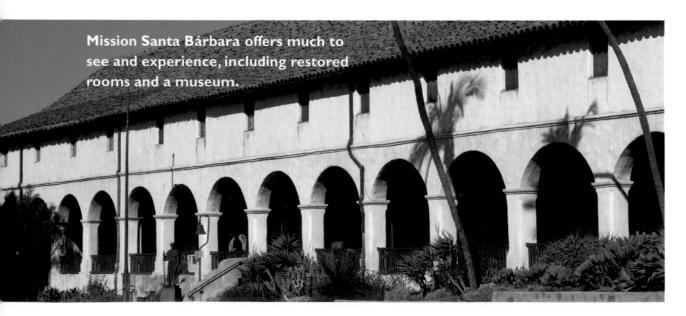

Mission Santa Bárbara offers much to see and experience, including restored rooms and a museum.

10
Make Your Own Mission Model

To make your own model of Mission Santa Bárbara, you will need:

- cardboard
- Foam Core board
- glue
- paint (red, tan, white)
- pencil
- Popsicle sticks
- ruler
- tape
- sand
- scissors
- red modeling clay

DIRECTIONS

Adult supervision is suggested.

Step 1: Cut a piece of Foam Core measuring 20"× 20" (50.8 × 50.8 cm) for the base of your mission. Mix tan paint with sand for texture, and paint the base with this mixture. Allow it to dry.

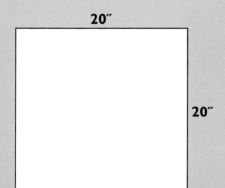

20″

20″

Step 2: Cut a 30"× 11" (76.2 × 27.9 cm) piece of cardboard for the church. On both sides, score three 3" (7.6-cm) sections lightly into the cardboard.

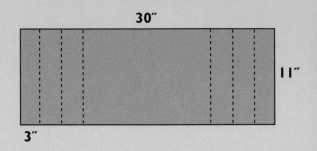

Step 3: In the center of the top edge of the cardboard, cut out a rectangle measuring 6"× 5" (15.2 × 12.7 cm).

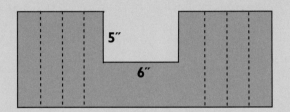

Step 4: Draw and then cut two arched windows at the top of each 3" (7.6-cm) section. Cut two more arched windows on either side of the cut-out square. Draw and then cut a door in the center of the bottom edge.

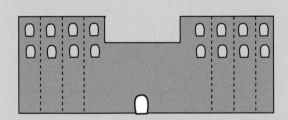

Step 5: Fold the cardboard to form the bell towers and the front of the church.

Step 6: Cut two 3"× 3" (7.6 × 7.6 cm) squares of cardboard. Glue both to the top of the bell towers. Add a dome made of clay to each.

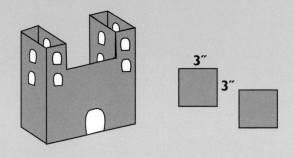

Step 7: From cardboard, cut two walls measuring 4"× 6" (10.2 × 15.2 cm). This will be the back of the church. Cut one square (for the rear wall) that measures 6"× 6" (15.2 × 15.2).

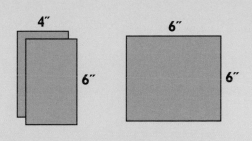

Step 8: To make the pointed roof of the church, cut two triangles that are 6" (15.2 cm) wide and 3" (7.6 cm) at the peak. Glue one to the top edge of the back wall and one between the bell towers.

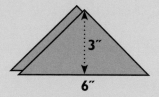

Step 9: Paint the Popsicle sticks red, and glue to the triangle to make the tiled roof.

Step 10: To make the friars' quarters, cut two 11"× 5" (27.9 × 12.7 cm) cardboard rectangles. These will be the front and back walls.

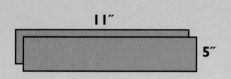

Step 11: Draw and the cut 10 arched doors. Draw and cut a small window above each door in one of the walls.

Step 12: Cut two 4"× 6.5" (10.2 × 16.5 cm) pieces of cardboard for the end walls of the friars' quarters. Then cut off the corners.

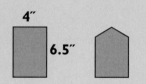

Step 13: Put the front, back, and end walls of the friars' quarters together, and tape the inside corners.

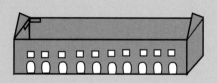

Step 14: To make the roof of the friars' quarters, cut an 11" × 5" (27.9 × 12.5 cm) piece of cardboard. Fold it lengthwise down the middle. Glue the roof to the top of the building. Allow it to dry.

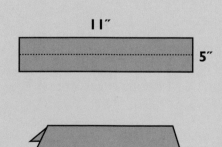

Step 15: Glue three thin strips of cardboard to each side of the door. Mix white paint with sand. Paint the mission with this mixture. Add trees and grass to the mission grounds.

The model of Mission Santa Bárbara when completed.

Key Dates in Mission History

1492	Christopher Columbus reaches the West Indies
1542	Cabrillo's expedition to California
1602	Sebastián Vizcaíno sails to California
1713	Fray Junípero Serra is born
1769	Founding of San Diego de Alcalá
1770	Founding of San Carlos Borroméo del Río Carmelo
1771	Founding of San Antonio de Padua and San Gabriel Arcángel
1772	Founding of San Luis Obispo de Tolosa
1775–76	Founding of San Juan Capistrano
1776	Founding of San Francisco de Asís
1776	Declaration of Independence is signed

1777	Founding of Santa Clara de Asís
1782	Founding of San Buenaventura
1784	Fray Serra dies
1786	Founding of Santa Bárbara
1787	Founding of La Purísima Concepción
1791	Founding of Santa Cruz and Nuestra Señora de la Soledad
1797	Founding of San José, San Juan Bautista, San Miguel Arcángel, and San Fernando Rey de España
1798	Founding of San Luis Rey de Francia
1804	Founding of Santa Inés
1817	Founding of San Rafael Arcángel
1823	Founding of San Francisco Solano
1833	Mexico passes Secularization Act
1848	Gold found in northern California
1850	California becomes the thirty-first state

Glossary

aqueduct (AH-kwuh-dukt) A manmade ditch that carries water from its source to another source, usually over long distances.

Christianity (kris-chee-A-nih-tee) The branch of religion based on the teachings of Jesus Christ and the Bible, practiced by Eastern, Roman Catholic, and Protestant groups.

convert (kun-VURT) To change from belief in one religion to the belief in another religion.

Franciscan (fran-SIS-kin) A communal Roman Catholic order of friars, or "brothers," who follow the teachings and examples of Saint Francis of Assisi.

friar (FRY-ur) A brother in a communal religious order. Friars can also be priests.

indigenous (inn-DIH-jen-us) A person, place, or thing that comes from a specific area.

Jesuit (JEZSH-yoo-it) A communal Roman Catholic order of priests who follow the teachings of Saint Ignatius of Loyola.

Las Californias (LAS kah-lee-FOR-nee-ahs) The name given by the Spanish Empire to the northwestern territory of New Spain.

livestock (LYV-stohk) Farm animals kept for use or profit.

missionary (MIH-shun-ayr-ee) A person who teaches his or her religion to people with different beliefs.

secularization (sehk-yoo-luh-rih-ZAY-shun) A process by which the mission lands were made to be nonreligious.

shaman (SHAH-min) A religious and spiritual leader who heals the sick through medicine and ritual.

tanning (TA-ning) The chemical treatment of raw animal hides or skins to convert them into leather.

tule (TOO-lee) A type of reed once used by Native Americans in the construction of houses and boats.

verdant (VER-dent) Green, healthy (usually referring to plants or vegetation).

Pronunciation Guide

atole (ah-TOH-lay)

fray (FRAY)

monjerío (mohn-hay-REE-oh)

pozole (poh-SOH-lay)

siesta (see-EHS-tah)

temescal (TEH-mes-kal)

tomol (TOH-mul)

Find Out More

To learn more about the California missions, check out these books, museums, and websites:

BOOKS

Behrens, June. *Central Coast Missions in California*. Minneapolis, MN: Lerner Publishing Group, 2007.

Hackel, Stephen W. *Junípero Serra: California's Founding Father*. New York, NY: Hill and Wang, 2013.

Gibson, Karen Bush. *Native American History for Kids*. Chicago, IL: Chicago Review Press, 2010.

O'Dell, Scott. *Island of the Blue Dolphins*. Chicago, IL: HMH Books for Young Readers, 2010.

MUSEUMS

Here are two places in the Santa Barbara area you might want to visit.

Mission Santa Bárbara
2201 Laguna Street
Santa Barbara, CA 93105
(805) 682-4713
www.santabarbaramission.org

The Santa Barbara Museum of Art

1130 State Street
Santa Barbara, CA 93101
(805) 963-4364
www.sbmuseart.org

WEBSITES

Santa Barbara Nature – Information on the Chumash

www.sbnature.org/research/anthro/chumash
Take a look inside the daily lives of the Chumash people, as well
as explore resources archived by the Santa Barbara Museum of
Natural History.

Santa Ynez Chumash Website

www.santaynezchumash.org
Explore more about the history, culture, and ancestry of the
Chumash people.

The Website of Mission Santa Bárbara

www.santabarbaramission.org
At each of the twenty-one Spanish missions along El Camino Real,
Franciscans established a protected orchard as well as gardens of
vegetables and flowers. Discover how La Huerta Historic Gardens
is a living museum of botanical heritage.

Index